no god no son of god 2

no god no son of god 2

James Russell Sarver, Sr.

To order additional copies of this book, contact:
Xlibris Corporation
1-888-795-4274
www.Xlibris.com
Orders@Xlibris.com
117840

CONTENTS

DEDICATION

this book is dedicated to Greg

Between 2 TV shows, there was a placard on the screen. It said that blue collar workers were down 60% and white collar workers were up 70%. In other words, this country is not doing anything but we are getting down on paper. That was at least 30 years ago. It has gotten much worst since then. You can bet your last dollar that will change if I get into power. Every possible way that paperwork can be stopped, I WILL STOP IT.

ASPARTAME AND
TED KENNEDY

Ted Kennedy is the perfect example of how the Kennedy Illegal Voting Machine can make a United States Senator out of a worthless piece of trash. This has happened all over the United States. Because of the Kennedy Illegal Voting Machine we have had worthless pieces of trash at every level of our government. This includes the House, the Senate, the Vice President, the President, and even the Justices of the Supreme Court. The Kennedy Illegal Voting Machine was developed by Joseph Patrick Kennedy, Sr. Millions of illegal votes had been cast. As far back as FDR, or possibly further, the democrats have used the Kennedy Illegal Voting Machine. FDR, Truman, JFK, LBJ, Carter, Clinton, and even Obama used the Kennedy Illegal Voting Machine to win their elections. I know what, when, where, why, and who. I just do not know how the Kennedys got these votes into our election system. In the election of 1960 there was somewhere near 20 million illegal votes cast for Kennedy and Johnson. There were over 100,000,000 votes cast. While the number of legal, live, registered voters was somewhere a little over 80,000,000. The computer had Nixon winning by 151/1 odds. The county in Kentucky who had voted for every President voted for Nixon. Nixon not only won the election, but he won by a landslide. In the 1948 election the headlines read that Dewey defeated Truman, and he did. However, it was the Kennedy Illegal Voting Machine that gave the election to Truman. In 1951 Truman fired General Douglass McArthur. In April of 1964 General Douglass McArthur passed away. I had never seen my mother cry, but I saw her cry that whole day. My mother drilled into me to actually hate Truman. The movie industry tried several times to make a movie about Truman. However, the hatred for Truman was just too great. On important issues my mother and I agreed, especially our great love and admiration for Richard M. Nixon. On things that did not matter my mother and I were at each other's throats constantly. She liked coke. I liked Pepsi. She liked the St. Louis Cardinals. I liked the New York Yankees It really make things colorful around the Sarver household. I was writing a letter in my mind's eye explaining to Richard M. Nixon how the Kennedys cheated to defeat him. Before I could get the letter down on paper and mailed to him he passed away. I was devastated. This was the reason for Watergate. Nixon knew that the democrats cheated. He just did not know how. The Kennedys were great at using illegal votes, but LBJ was the greatest ever. LBJ used dead voters. He and Conley were even caught on tape getting names off of tombstones. WARNING: Watch out for the New Madrid Fault System. From Dec, 1811 to the middle of 1812 there were over 2,000 earthquakes, tremors, and aftershocks along this large area. Some of these faults are the deepest on earth. According to the experts when this erupts again 6 major cities will be destroyed. Two of which are Evansville and Memphis. I do not remember the others. The Mississippi River ran backwards and made a new bed when it came back down. Some land turned to quick sand. Plaster cracked and church bells rang as far away as Boston and Montreal. It is not a question of if. It is a question of when. Two scientists wrote a book. I believe the title is The Quakes That America Forgot. It is the greatest book that I have ever read. The New Madrid Fault System could go off tomorrow. or it could happen 200 to 500 years from now. I am just trying to let people know.

Amendment To Aspartame And Ted Kennedy

I almost forgot why I wrote my last article. We had a petition signed, sealed, and delivered against Aspartame. We were Winning big time. Ted Kennedy stopped us. If it had not been for the Kennedy Illegal Voting Machine Ted Kennedy would have never been a Senator. We would have gotten Aspartame banned.

THE PERFECT EXAMPLE

Ted Kennedy is the perfect example of what happens when the Kennedy Illegal Voting Machine makes a United States Senator out of a worthless piece of trash. This has happened all on over is country. Because of the Kennedy Illegal Voting Machine the United States has had worthless pieces of trash at every level of the government.

Two Kennedy Truths

Ted and Mary Jo were parked along the road. A state police officer pulled up behind them. He got out of his car merely to check on them. Mary Jo jumped into the driver's seat and took off. She stopped quickly to let Ted out of the car. Mary Jo went over the bridge and into the water by herself. JFK, Jr. killed a girl. He was choking her, using this to make their sex better. The police did not arrest him because she told him to do it. In other words, l could have a g gun in my hand. You could tell me to shoot you, and I could not be arrested because you told me to do it. It really sickens me that the Kennedys have gotten by with so much. A bonus Michael Kennedy Smith got by with rape because he was too good-looking and could not rape anyone.

THE INTELLIGENT AMERICAN PEOPLE

I could not figure out how The Intelligent American People could vote for the likes of FDR, Truman, Kennedy, Johnson, Carter, Clinton, and Obama. I had lost all faith in the American People. Now, that faith has returned because I know that they did not vote for any of these men. All of these men were elected by the Kennedy Illegal Voting Machine. In order for a republican to win they must first beat millions of votes from the Kennedy Illegal Voting Machine. As I look back it is easy for me to see that it takes a republican to win in order to fix the screw-ups that the democrats created. Eisenhower had this country in the best shape that it has ever been. It took Kennedy and Johnson several years to ruin what Eisenhower had done. I believe that Obama will win this election because the democrats will once again use the Kennedy Illegal Voting Machine.

The Ultimate Depression

It does not matter who wins the election. A severe depression is inevitable. This depression will be the worst depression ever on earth. The reason why this depression shall be so terrible is most Americans are pansies and pussies. They cannot handle even the slightest hardships. There will be no heat. There will be no electricity. There will be no gasoline for their cars. There will be mass starvation and mass suicide. I did my best to stop it. I screamed at www.xlibris.com to get my book no god no son of god published in June 2012. I may have had time to get the book promoted. All of the answers are in that book. I see no way to get my book to the people. One night you will go to sleep. The next day the dollar will not be worth one thin dime.

THE GREAT SPIRIT

Many people have told me that there must be a supreme being. They are correct. That supreme being is The Great Spirit according to the Tribes of Turtle Island. I will attempt to explain this to you. Look, Jim. Look at the TV, Jim. Do you see it, Jim? Yes, I see it. Listen, Jim. Listen to the radio, Jim. Do you hear it, Jim? Yes? Yes, I hear it. Read the book, Jim. Do you understand it, Jim? Yes, I understand it. Time and time and time again I have been shown things by The Great Spirit. That is how I was able to write no god no son of god. The Tribes of Turtle have always been right. They are without a doubt the greatest society ever on earth, and they have all of the right answers. To me The Great Spirit is called Mother Nature. The earth, sun, waters, animals, and plants hold the truth of everything that controls mankind. There is no god. There never was a god, and there will never be a god, only The Great Spirit or Mother Nature. You can make the call.

THE GREAT SPIRIT
OR MOTHER NATURE

I thought that I wrote no god no son of god all by myself. Now, I know that there was a co-author. The Tribes of Te Island call the supreme being The Great Spirit. The white man calls the supreme being Mother Nature. The Great Spirit or Mother Nature is extremely mad. Chemicals are destroying the earth, water, and air. The use of chemical fertilizer, pesticides, and herbicides by our farmers is absolutely horrible. Households are using chemical soaps and other dangerous chemicals. The Great Spirit or Mother Nature is about to bring down pure havoc on the United States and Great Britain like nobody has ever seen before. I can only advise you to start using Shaklee Products. Shaklee Products will bring back the quality of our earth, water, and even the air.

ALUMINUM POISONING

As far as I know all cigarettes and all cigarette tobaccos are packed in aluminum. That means that every time I take a drag off of my cigarette I suck aluminum into my lungs. Aluminum is a dangerous chemical to both plants and animals. You should not drink out of an aluminum can. You should not cook in an aluminum pan. You should not cover food with aluminum foil. Again, Aluminum is a dangerous chemical. I believe that it is aluminum that is causing the cancer blamed on tobacco products. One more time, ALUMINUM IS A DANGEROUS CHEMICAL!!!

STUPID!

One woman told me that Romney said he was going to lower Social Security, Medicare, and Medicaid on purpose, and that he lost the election intentionally. This may seem absurd, but put the shoe on the other foot. The biggest groups of voters were the baby boomers and the elderly. I challenge all Americans to come up with any kind of logical reason that Romney chose this absolutely stupid move. This is the second election in a row where the American People just plain did not have a choice. Tell me why the republican party cannot come up with a decent candidate. Isn't there even one republican that is worth considering? If you want to cure an ailing economy you do not start at the bottom. You start at the top. The first topic on my agenda was to be the seat belt law. However, that has been pre empted by my younger son, Sgt. Jason Wayne Wilson, of the Indiana National Guard. We all know that Congress gives themselves a raise every time they turn around. This would stop, and stop now. The President would give raises to the Justices of the Supreme Court. The Justices of the Supreme Court would give raises to Congress, and the Congress would give raises to the President This would be our balance of powers working perfectly. Sgt. Wilson told me that Congress, the President, and I do not know who else continues to get their salaries after they have left office. That would stop, and stop now. The only Federal Government Officials that would continue to get their salaries after they have left their office would be the Justices of the Supreme Court. They were appointed for life. They will be paid for life. Furthermore the salaries of all Federal Government Officials with the exception of the Justices of the Supreme Court shall be sliced in half. Then we will find out who wants to represent the people or who are in politics only for the money. This is where you start when you want to cure an ailing economy.

Romney Wins

Contest the results of the election. Every democrat President since FOR, and maybe earlier, have used illegal votes to win their elections. FOR, Truman, Kennedy, Johnson, Carter, Clinton, and even Obama have used illegal votes to win. There were nearly 20 million illegal votes cast for Kennedy and Johnson in 1960.The headlines read that Dewey defeated Truman, and he did. Joseph Patrick Kennedy, Sr developed the Kennedy Illegal Voting Machne. I do not know how Kennedy got the illegal votes into the system. All I know is that he did. All of the experts said that Ted Kennedy would lose his last election. He used the Kennedy Illegal Voting Machine to win.

George W. H. Bush

It has been 49 years ago since JFK was killed. The man who killed him was Lucien Sarti. Sarti said that I killed your President. Get over it. George W. H Bush was walking around the streets of Dallas. Wasn't George W. H. Bush the Director of the CIA? Somebody needs to ask George W. H. Bush what he was doing just walking the streets of Dallas. You know, somebody needs to ask George W. H. Bush what the Director of the CIA was doing just walking around the streets of Dallas. It has been a long time. I would guess that Bush thinks he got by with it. Who would think that an old amateur scientist specializing in chemistry and the American Family would figure it all out? Do you want to tell the people George, or would you rather that I tell them? I have written this e-mail because I believe that there are a lot of low people in high places that want to kill me. I know too much for my own safety.

Lucien Sarti

Lucien Sarti is the man who shot and killed JFK. He shot JFK from a manhole. One bullet hit JFK in the small of his throat and exited out the back of his head. Another bullet hit JFK in the chest Either bullet would have probably killed JFK. Lucien said, "I killed your President. Get over it". 1 have not proved it yet, but I believe that Sarti was a Russian sniper. Russia and Cuba were afraid of JFK. This was mainly caused by the Cuban Missile Crisis. JFK had made this great big statement about what he would do if Russia did not get rid of those missiles in Cuba. JFK even sent, not one, but two aircraft carriers down to Cuba to show off his power. However, two weeks before this JFK made a compromise with Russia that we would get rid of certain missiles in strategic places. Russia would get rid of the ones in Cuba. Still, the Russians and Cubans were afraid of JFK. That is why the Russians and the Cubans were in on the death of JFK. Again, Earl Warren was a communist, and when LBJ returned to his office there was a note on his desk telling him to allow Earl Warren to investigate the death of JFK. I just as well tell you that Jackie was in on the death of her husband. Jackie was sick and tired of hearing that JFK slept with this woman and JFK slept with that woman. Supposedly, Jackie went after the piece of John's head. She went the wrong way. Then the story was that Jackie was trying to pull the secret service man into the limo. The truth was that the secret service man was trying to push Jackie back into the limo. Bullets were raining from everywhere. Jackie was trying to save her own skin.

Prove Or Disprove

George W. H. Bush and the CIA were in on the death of JFK. Lucien Sarti was The man who shot and killed JFK. Sarti was a Russian sniper. He said, "I killed your President. Get over it". I only have one item left to prove or disprove was organized crime in on it. I have heard all kinds of rumors, but I have no real truth.

SOMEBODY

John F. Kennedy never had a prayer. Bullets were fired at him from all directions. Shots were fired by Lee Harvey Oswald. Shots were fired at him from the Grassy Knoll. Shots were fired at him from George W. H. Bush and the CIA. And shots were fired at him from Lucien Sarti, a Russian sniper. If he could have avoided the bullets from Sarti he might be alive today. Somebody needs to ask George W. H. Bush why he was walking around the streets of Dallas that day. Somebody need ask the Director of the CIA what he was doing walking around the streets that day, Nov.22, 1963. Come on George. You can tell them. It has been Forty-nine years. Come on, George. Earl Warren was a communist. The Warren Report was to put the blame on Oswald so the Russians would not get the blame. I believe that the conspiracy to kill Kennedy involved 100 individuals or more. Sarti hit JFK with two bullets. One bullet hit Kennedy in the chest. The other bullet hit the small of his throat and exiled out of the back of his head. Either bullet would have been fatal. Questions—With bullets coming from everywhere how is it that no innocent bystanders were killed? How could 100 men, or more, keep such a terrible and tragic incident a secret for forty-nine years? Is Sarti still alive, and if so, should Sarti be prosecuted for the murder of John F. Kennedy? This incident would have started WW3.It was the death of one man that started WW1. WW3 would have been between Russia and the United States Armageddon. Somebody would have pushed the Big Red Button. The earth, plants, and all animals would have perished. Somebody would have pushed the Big Red Button. Somebody would have pushed the Big Red Button. Somebody.

Not Out
Of The Woods Yet

Years ago the United Nations made a committee. The only purpose of this committee was to make certain that no nations from the Middle East or any other undeveloped country was able to get nuclear capabilities, such as North Korea. After several years the only individuals on this committee were from the very nations that the committee was suppose to stop. Now, Iran and North Korea have nuclear capabilities. We are not out of the woods yet, and the number of nations having these capabilities are only going to get higher. Every day we get closer to some idiot leader pushing the Big Red Button—THE END OF THE WORLD

To My Librarian Friend, Greg

I trust that you have read Not Out Of The Woods Yet. I read this article in Reader's Digest 20 to 30 years ago. The terrible has happened. Iran and North Korea now have nuclear capabilities. One wrong move in this chess match, you will have check mate . . . . The End Of The World. Some will believe that they are safe in their bomb shelters. Not True! The radioactivity will be so strong all over the world that all people will die the instant they come out of their shelters. Because of this radioactivity no known life will be able to exist for hundreds, maybe even thousands, of years . . . . BOO! Iran or North Korea just hit the Big Red Button.

MISS C. SHARP

I trust that you read Not Out Of The Woods Yet. I read the article in the Reader's Digest 20-30 years ago. The terrible has happened. Iran and North Korea now have nuclear capabilities. One wrong move in this chess match, and you will have check mate, The End Of The World. Some people will believe that they are safe in their bomb shelters. Not True-The radiation will be so intense that these people will die as soon as they come out of their bomb shelters. It will take a few days for Iran and/or North Korea to get the bombs ready. So, you will have time to pray. As far as the election goes Obama received 1,000,000 illegal votes from the Kennedy Illegal Voting Machine in the states of NY, IL, TX, CA, OH, and PA. Romney won the election by a landslide, just as Kennedy used illegal votes to defeat Nixon. Obama used illegal votes to defeat McCain. Even I spaced one election. That was the Carter and Ford election. I believed as everybody else believed, that Carter won because Ford pardoned Nixon. That was also false The Kennedy Illegal Voting Machine was used by the democrats so it appeared that Carter won. I lost all faith in the American People in 1964 when Johnson won the election. Again, it was illegal votes that won for Johnson. The Kennedys were great at using illegal votes, but Johnson was the greatest ever. Johnson used illegal dead voters, and he was actually caught on tape getting names off of tombstones. Johnson lost one election by less than 1,000 votes, but he could not contest this election because his illegal votes would have shown up. FDR, Truman, Kennedy, Johnson, Carter, Clinton, and even Obama used illegal votes to win their elections. To me, it is a miracle that we even have a country. The worst thing that ever happened to the American People was the 1964 Civil Rights Act. Employers could only hire inexperienced women and blacks. The quantity of American products went to hell. The quality went to shit Our products were the laughing stock of the whole world. Men could not find jobs to support their families, and there was mass divorce. Integration and bussing was horrible. We just as well put our kids in schools, blocked all the doors and windows and turned loose starving Siberian tigers through the coal shoots. This could not have caused any more problems. The songs, The Cat's In The Cradle and Skip A Rope were my generation screaming out in pain because of the !964 Civil Rights Act. Even though Kennedy was dead his goal of having free sex became a reality. Women became sluts and whores You could turn their pussies inside out, and they would look like a pin cushion. Listen to the children as they play. Listen to the children and what the say. Well, Johnny, I wonder who will be sleeping with Mommy tonight. I don't know, but I bet it will not be Daddy. As the song says, And Mommy and Daddy are who's to blame. That is wrong. They may be separated or even divorced, but you can bet your bottom dollar that every one of them loved their children. Who was to blame? THE DEMOCRAT PARTY! What was to blame? The 1964 CIVIL RIGHTS ACT. You will never believe what saved the American Family. Any teenager can tell you.

To Steer And Steer

First, let me thank you for being a friend. I wondered why I felt so warm inside looking at your Christmas decorations. It finally dawned on me when I bought Sam's Christmas present. For the first time since I was 12 years old I had the Christmas Spirit. Mom and Dad bought their first artificial tree. Mom had her new movie camera which contained these huge spot lights. You could barely see they were so bright. My two siblings (Beth had just been born in November) had to wear pajamas. We never wore anything but our underwear. We all received many presents, but I just did not enjoy any of them. So, thank you for allowing Sam and I into your lives. You know that I am big into the political and government world. This takes me into something that concerns you. That is homosexualism.It is here to stay, and through my studies I have learned that it is just as natural as heterolism. (sp).The only unnatural thing is when it is caused by Aspartame Poisoning. It does not matter whether a baby has a dick or a pussy. It is the hormones that control the sexual world. Parents who have consumed products containing Aspartame are the cause here. My real concern is simple. I want homosexuals to come up with their own terminology. The "normal people" gave male homosexuals the name, Queers. I find this name disgusting. Instead of Queers why not call yourselves Steers. Surely, you have heard the joke, there is nothing but Steers and Queers in Texas, and you don't have any horns. Instead of saying that you are going to get married, how about saying that you are going to get hitched. I think you get the idea. You can come up with your own ideas. I sincerely believe that homosexuals should have the same rights as the "normal people" because they are just as normal. Come up with your own terminology, and I will fight on your side. I was walking down the street in Crawfordsville, IN, with a buddy. Two beautiful girls walked by. I said to my buddy boy, I sure would like some of that. My buddy said Jim you don't want any of that, they are lesbians. I said what is a lesbian. He said they like pussy. I said, well, I must be a lesbian too.

DEATH BY
ASPARTAME POISONING

Twenty-seven are dead, caused by Aspartame Poisoning. Proof? I do not need any proof. I am 64 years old. I have seen what Aspartame can do. American soldiers are deathly sick. One out of eight women have breast cancer. There are more women dead than men due to Lung Cancer. Sugar Diabetes is an epidemic, along with Lupus, and M.S. None of these things were true when I was a teenager. Aspartame affects the brain and causes humans to do strange things, such as what just happened. The Columbine Shootings and the many Sniper Shootings were also caused by Aspartame Poisoning. Drivers are having accidents, and they have no idea what happened. Well . . . . I know what happens. It is called Aspartame Poisoning! Normal people do not do these things, only those affected by Aspartame.

I WILL NEVER FORGET

I must have told my daughter at least 100 times not to drink diet Pepsi. She had 7 miscarriages. Her doctor told her to quit drinking diet Pepsi for at least one year before trying again. The doctor must have had a guilty conscience because he confided in her. He told my daughter that he knew that diet Pepsi caused every one of her miscarriages. He told her that he was not supposed to tell anyone that Aspartame is dangerous. I do not know where that order came from, but I do know that it was a bribe. I pleaded with my daughter. I told her that her Daddy told her many times to not drink diet Pepsi. I Will NEVER FORGET HER WORDS TO ME . . . . DADDY, YOU ARE NOT A DOCTOR.

ANCESTRY

I have known since before I was twelve years old that the Sarver and Stultz families are at least part tribal. I knew this because of the way my father treated my mother. There is no race of people on earth that treats their women like the Tribes Of Turtle Island (you call Indians and Columbus called Indios, meaning god-like).I studied my Grandpa Sarver first. His name was C. Earl Serber. He changed his name to Earl C. Sarver. Grandpa was born on Sept.18, 1891. I was born on Sept. 18, 1948.Thecomputer showed pictures of Grandpa when he was younger. I was shocked. My own mother could have not known whether it was Grandpa or me. Grandpa was pure Swiss. Grandma Sarver was named Eva Ethel (Keller) Sarver. The Sarvers were from Virginia. The Kellers got mixed up with the Lees, and the computer puked out that I was a grandson of General Robert Edward Lee. I Had already guessed that. Grandpa Stultz's name was Roy Ulysses Stultz (have you guessed it yet?) Yes, I had already figured it out, but I had no real proof. On Christmas Eve 2012my uncle, Robert Stultz drove me to my sister's house for the Sarver Christmas celebration. He told me that Grandpa had told him many times that Grandpa was named after Ulysses Simpson Grant (whose real name was Hiram Ulysses Grant). Hence, my nickname, Hiram Horatio "Boar" Hog. That was enough for me. I am the oldest living relative of both, General Grant and General Lee. By the way, the Stultzs and the Grants were from Ohio. Now, they are attempting to find out if I am related to Crazy Horse. If I find out that I am related to Crazy Horse, I will be impossible to live with. The U.S.is in extremely terrible shape! I can straighten it out. I would have to be declared a Dictator/President with Sara Palin as my Vice President for four years. Sara would appoint an all new Supreme Court. She would also appoint my entire cabinet with the exception of the head of the FDA (which would be Dr. Betty Martini. Dr. Martini would be the only cabinet member allowed to use men) Sara would also appoint the FBI, CIA, Secret Service; etc.AII of these would be republican women. The

League Of Women Voters would fill the seat of the House Of Representatives and the Senate with more republican women. The men have screwed up the government completely. Women are not controlled by power but are literally by their maternal instinct, just like the women of the Tribes Of Turtle Island. Therefore, they make much better leaders.

THE REVEREND JIM SERVER

Rev. Martin Luther King, Rev. Jesse Jackson, Malcolm, and just about every other black leader never believed in God. They just used God to get what they wanted. Nearly every black all the way back to slaves' times never believed in God. Do you have any idea just how easy it Is to get the title of Reverend in front of your name? It is a little late today, but by tomorrow or for sure the next day I could easily be Reverend Jim Sarver. I could use the computer, mall order, radio, TV, or just about any source, and nobody would contest it. It Is just that easy. I have always cried because I have known since before I was twelve years old that the Blacks only used God to get what they wanted. Like just about everything that I am able to see it is just so easy to see all the things that God has been used for.

The Reverend Jim Sarver

THE DANGERS OF SMOKING

The most dangerous thing is that cigarettes are packed in aluminum. Aluminum is extremely dangerous to both plants and animals. You should not drink out of an aluminum can. You should not cook in aluminum. In my agenda I say that smoking will not be allowed in any enclosed area.lt would be nearly impossible to enforce this law as far as homes and vehicles. l would beg you to not smoke in your homes and vehicles if you have children under the age of 25, non-smokers in your homes or vehicles, or you have pets. It will be illegal to pack cigarettes in any metal. The next most dangerous thing is menthol cigarettes. If you really want to die smoke menthol cigarettes. Your lungs will look like sponges, and you will literally drown in your own liquid. Almost as dangerous as the first two is sitting in front of a TV 24/7 smoking and drinking coffee or beer. This will cause death whether you are smoking or not. I was to be in a test with Purdue University. I was to smoke as many cigarettes as possible within a certain amount of time. I was unable to take the test because my lungs were more clear than any of their non-smokers. This is how doctors and hospitals can say that tobacco causes cancer. They use people who have one foot on a banana and the other one in the grave. More women die from lung cancer than men. Men are starting to live longer: than women. Men smoke way more cigarettes than women. So, it is high time to look for another cause for lung cancer. As a matter of fact it is time to look for another cause of all cancers. The answer is simple. The cause is Aspartame Poisoning. Many more women consume products containing Aspartame I cannot resist. I just cannot resist. Why are Americans FAT? The answer to that question is so simple that a child should be able to figure it out. Americans are fat because THEY DO NOT WALK!!!!!!!!! Americans have to drive two blocks to get a loaf of bread or a gallon of milk. Years ago children walked miles one way to school. Today they just walk out the front door and step into a waiting bus. Steve Reeves invented Power Walking. You put a little weight on each wrist. You put a little weight on each ankle, and you put a little weight around your big belly. Take off walking with as long of strides as are comfortable. The heel to heel stride burns more fat calories by percentage than any other exercise known to mankind. Pick out the total number of miles that you want to walk, and divide this figure in half. Walk this in one half. Turnaround and walk back home That way you are always, always, always coming home. You can even make this a family affair, or you can walk with a friend or friends. NEVER<NEVER<NEVER JOG. That damages every bone cartilage, muscle, brain, etc. of your body. I went out of my mind when the jogging craze hit America. NEVER, NEVER, NEVER JOG. If you truly want to lose weight try POWER WALKING.

NOTES

NOTES

NOTES

NOTES

NOTES

NOTES

NOTES

NOTES

NOTES

NOTES

NOTES

NOTES

NOTES

www.ingramcontent.com/pod-product-compliance
Lightning Source LLC
Chambersburg PA
CBHW050345290526
45785CB00006B/2649